Wearable Brain Books

"Knowledge at the speed of thought"

David Gomadza

www.twofuture.world

PAPERBACK ISBN: 9798323522620

DEDICATION

A better more interesting future.

CONTENTS

1 WHAT ARE WEARABLE BRAIN BOOKS? 1

ACKNOWLEDGMENTS

To Tomorrow's World Order

WHAT ARE WEARABLE BRAIN BOOKS?

The Future of Reading is Here: Wearable Brain Books.

"Knowledge at the speed of thought"

Imagine accessing information at the speed of thought, feeling the emotions of every word, and storing countless books in your mind. Wearable brain books, a revolutionary new technology, turn this science fiction into reality.

Here is how this works.

Brain-Computer Interface: These books are digital databases uploaded directly into your brain.

Multiple Books, One Mind: Upload up to 9 books simultaneously and access them all instantly.

Brain Command Control: Use your thoughts to upload, read, save, and remove books. No more flipping pages!

Feel the Words: Experience stories in a whole new way. Books convert words into emotions you can feel through nerve impulses.

Why Wearable Brain Books Are the Future:

Unparalleled Speed: Access information instantly, surpassing the limitations of traditional reading.
Emotional Connection: Feel the depth of every story with a deeper emotional connection to the text.
Effortless Learning: Store vast amounts of knowledge directly in your brain for easy recall.
Personalized Experience: The system adapts to your gender for a customized reading experience.

How to Get Started:

First say silently in your brain;

My voice is my password

My brain is my reader

Then

1. Choose a book and get its unique code. Eg
2. Command your brain to "Upload & Read."
3. Feel the story come alive as your brain processes the information.

This is more than just reading - it's an immersive experience. Wearable brain books have the potential to transform education, entertainment, and the way we access information. With this revolutionary technology, the future of reading is not just imagined, it's in your hands (or rather, your mind).
Don't be left behind. Embrace the future of knowledge and pre-order your wearable brain book today!

Beyond the Basics: Unveiling the Full Potential of Wearable Brain Books

We've unveiled the core concept of wearable brain books, but there's a whole universe of possibilities waiting to be explored. Here's a deeper dive into what this technology holds:

Democratizing Knowledge:

Imagine a world where language barriers are broken. Wearable brain books could translate information in real-time, allowing anyone to access knowledge regardless of their native tongue.

Personalized Learning:

This technology isn't a one-size-fits-all solution. Learning styles and paces could be accommodated by adjusting the presentation of information. Visual learners could experience stories in vivid imagery, while auditory learners might hear the text come alive in their minds.

Enhanced Memory:

Wearable brain books could potentially act as memory enhancers. By directly storing information, they could revolutionize studying and knowledge retention.

Accessibility for All:

This technology has the potential to bridge the gap for individuals with visual impairments or reading difficulties. Wearable brain books could open up a whole new world of literature and learning for everyone.

Ethical Considerations:

As with any groundbreaking technology, ethical considerations need to be addressed. Privacy concerns surrounding information stored within the brain and potential inequalities in access are crucial aspects to consider.

The Future is Collaborative:

The development of wearable brain books is likely to be a collaborative effort between neuroscientists, engineers, ethicists, and even authors. Working together, they can ensure this technology benefits all of humanity.

The Bottom Line:

Wearable brain books are more than just a new way to read. They represent a paradigm shift in how we access and interact with information. It's a future filled with endless possibilities, and the journey has just begun. Are you ready to join the exploration?

Wearable Brain Books: A Sneak Peek at the First Editions

A glimpse into what the first editions are like:

Thoughts to Word Or Audio

The Learning Library:

Anyone can upload our best selling series directly into their brains. Complex concepts could be broken down and visualized for easier comprehension. Anyone can learn how the brain works with much easy.

The Interaction Aspect.

Everyone has an opportunity to interact with their brain through our wearable books. You can ask to talk to your brain and gain access into the world of your brain all this through a simple lines of brain commands.

You can therefore interact with your brain asking questions again using simple brain commands

First you can easily say:

My voice is my password.

[Now choose what you want to do one task at a time]

Either for reading

My brain is my reader

Or to analyze

My brain is my analyzer

The Diagnosis Analysts

My brain is my diagnosis specialist

[see Case Study at the end of the book.]

The Skill Shelf:

Learning a new language, mastering a musical instrument, or picking up a new hobby could be revolutionized. Wearable brain books could offer interactive experiences that guide you through the learning process, complete with simulations and real-time feedback.

The Empathy Experience:

Imagine feeling the emotions of historical figures as you delve into biographies, or experiencing the world through the eyes of a fictional character. Wearable brain books could foster deeper understanding and connection through emotional resonance.

The Customized Collection:

Your brain becomes the ultimate curator. Wearable brain books could personalize content based on your interests and learning style. Imagine a travel database that tailors information to your preferred destinations or a fitness database that customizes workout routines based on your goals.

The Evolving Editions:

With constant advancements, wearable brain books could become self-updating. Imagine a history database that seamlessly integrates new discoveries or a medical database that provides access to the latest research in real-time.

A Word on Safety:

The safety and security of this technology are paramount. Early wearable brain books might come with limitations on the amount of data uploaded or require user authentication for information retrieval. As the technology matures, ensuring privacy and preventing unauthorized access will be crucial.

The Future Beckons:

Wearable brain books represent a revolutionary leap forward in human-information interaction. While the initial editions might focus on specific applications, the potential for this technology is boundless. It's a future where learning becomes a seamless experience, and knowledge is truly at your fingertips (or rather, at your thoughts).

POTENTIAL.USE OF OUR WEARABLE BRAIN BOOKS AS A MEDICAL DIAGNOSIS SPECIALIST / FUTURE PREDICTOR OR SORCERER

Wearable Brain Books

Medical Diagnosis Specialist
A closer look at [Unknown] looking through her eyes through a Google search that retains her photos we retained the first report that calculated a vital signs report that indicated that at the time in question roughly on 25 September 2023 she was great and full of beans All her vitals were above 50 % here are the results
1 organs 99 % health
2 breathing was 78 % health
3 asintiser that measures lungs was above 95 %
4 weight was around 78 % bodmass
5 chest signs of life - she had nothing to ask about
6 she was happy and looking forward to life
7 she had a 99 % rate to live after 100 years
8 she had perfect DNA sequence recorded as ACTACTACTACTACTACT meaning close to goddess Catitighit meaning in super health
9 she had no damaged DNA stands
10 she was overall great and doing fine
11 she had no cervical cancers or any signs
12 she had no signs of vaginal cancer or anything pointing to this
13 she had no fallopian tube cancer
14 she was the happiest woman ever with a happiness score of 178 measured as how happy one can be out of 200 200 being happy and 0 being sad
15 she had no malignant tumor in her head
16 she was optimistic
17 she loved life
18 she wanted to be a princess officially [I want to stand and say I am the princess you have loved forever so love me now or let me...]

The second look in the eyes of an image taken on 27 March 2024 tells a complete different story unless it's Sabotage there is no medical condition that can explain this here are her vitals on this day [but could be just for that day but ...shocking]
1 organs are irreparably damaged
2 breathing is not normal it is irrestuvoc meaning can start but can stop unaccounted for [likely cause is acetate hromnopqrstuvwxyz meaning dancing inside the breathing place]
3 she had no issues at all but the Wearable Brain Book my brain is the diagnosis specialist retained a different verdict
a. She has suffered stage 2 trauma meaning life already reduced by 50 %
b. She had merntrstuvwxyz meaning early stage old age that can further reduce her life by 10 years on top of the 50 % above
c she is suffering from an incident as vital body organs attack that can result in dead in less than a year
d she is to be cut and something removed from here to stop this spreading but the cutting is to remove all her sources of fighting all lined up diseases so that she can't fight back when all set in
e she has level two ... that makes her scared of death enough to kill herself
f she has level two amnesia meaning she is scared of being scared
g she is noted as having addiction to pointing fingers at others
h she is noted as being arrogant about life and old age
I she has stage two vulnerability to fear
Now let's continue
4 she is now diagnosed as having advanced stage cancer of the cervix that if not treated will develop to vagina and fallopian tunes [?- arro- gance where gance is the conditioning by the queen where she must die for the queen [all this as a recipe for death made by her Majesty the queen Elizabeth on 28 June 17]
Can this be stopped and reversed?
We can therefore conclude that this is like a curse that befalls anyone who wants to take the throne for the queen
But the queen is dead?
Meaning seat must be empty
I object [I raised her from the dark place she was and she is in a better place that removes the curse- is someone manually apply all this and with what motive?]
If we look at the ordnance used 078986723 only true love can remove this curse but only the curse of death for the Majesty is

God's representative of God here on earth.
5 she was very healthy but now all vital signs have changed here is a list of all recorded vitals
1 now she has cancer of the fastest acting code 7282387648210 with no antidote created by NHS best specialist NB no one can beat this doctor in making lethal
2 she has damaged DNA sequence and here is a separate list
a code 7283849876832 worn out [labeled as the antimonarchy DNA sequence is caused by code 7983586789821 that redirects the protein needed to stop it being malnutritioned the antidote is 72812838782980 these are the codes for this
Ask.why
Ask.when
Ask.how
Nowaskwhy.start
This is because monarchies must be protected at any cost therefore must be always be in a position to kill their enemies hence the lack of a reversible DNA sequence but we can see that humans wrote this code and if we Ask the gods they believe we can change back this malicious code using code 72812838782980
If we Ask what else can be done then this code is the one used to ask everyone if they want a monarchy [clone 8 billion 7281238789292 and send to all true British people]
Now Ask what can be done and the answer is that these people are the true love she seeks not another husband these are the people who must vote how by asking it [7281238789292] to vacate the premises instead and follow queen to the holding place [xyzxhatstuvwzyaj
If we Ask why this is because this key I the one that commands everything in this case her life to death [all the people have to say is "that they all in one voice one greater than the Queen's - they love her"
Now let's Ask what else can be done
She can be made extra strong meaning code 72687958268 can be found and be used to activate other enzymes to fight along inside as well the codes are
Ask.why
Ask.when
Ask.how
Ask.howandwhy
Ask.whatif

That means the queen must answer
The answer that she is the queen and can never be replaced not by a ghost
What can be seen is that the seat of the queen is cursed and the curse must be removed by someone powerful than the queen herself through some self defense act
Now let's see what that might be
This could be someone greater than the queen herself who will say I am taking over this will automatically stop everything and breathing new life in the monarchy
If we are to watch to the end what will happen this is what is set to happen
1 she will die on 28 March 2025
2 she will suffer until her death a horrible death the most imaginable
3 she will forever surrender the role of princess
4 she will ask why everyday to buy time or the time will be reduced greatly
5 she will have everything removed when she is alive
6 she will have the vagina cut in preparation for her sacrifice
7 she will have part of the cervix removed
8 she will ask when everyday because the pain will be out of this world
9 she will try to end her life but fail because she loves life
10 she will forever die a painful death
11 she will lose all hair chemotherapy in the vagina will leave it skinhead
12 the chemotherapy in the head will remove her head
13 she will not have sex until the day she died to match the queen
14 she will whatif several. Times until it makes no sense
15 she will teach others how to behave among royal palace when real pain sets in in the ha ds of the royals enemies
17 she will ask why a billion times something the gods want to show humans power
18 she will not sleep as they will deliberately in the name of medical treatment remove the sleep switch to make sleeplessness
19 she will run everytime from the person she is with because everytime she runs they will gain coverage in papers etc. [Dr. Alamos who killed the queen meaning starting this loved cycle when they took power off the royals in the most cruel form possible

20 All this for medical. Purpose [just to show arrogance in the doctor's and their justification unless someone can find God and stop this then they are the most powerful because they took the crown from the royals and will take all the royals one by one with no one to stop this Antiroyals will love the doctors but the starts a cycle of revenge attacks when the doctors themselves identifies everything who benefited from all this and use the royals' pain to kill all. Using nothing but cancer

21 The royals must hand the doctors all the money they have as ransom and this means the doctors have power to hold all royals at ransom and the public with nothing to do but watch and if anyone who voice concern at the harsh punishment they will simply say do you know how many people the royals have killed? That alone will set a motion that will keep the doctors Klinger all royals so to save them is to let them die until the circle stops

22 whatif is the only option available but as we have seen the royals are tainted by the blood of everyone making them the least likely people who will try to challenge the doctors

23 Now it means waves change are on the rise is it time the doctors face justice because only God can stop the cycle I am now the real representative of Yahweh God on earth does that mean the end of the cycle of murder and walking away and getting away by the doctors.

Now if we Ask who on earth can stop this this is the answer No one even I [David Gomadza] can't protect anyone this is [9] royals will never accept a black person to be royal even if you are the only solution

Now we can see that the process is meant to weaken the royals for 200 years because after killing everyone for the next 200 years the royals DNA sequence will become assigned and determined by the deaths to self preserve meaning next two generations will. Be afraid of the do tors until this scared DNA is lost

What would this change everything possibly dismantle the royals as we know them today and stop funding their lovious spending if we Ask why is it because they can't get value for money from the royals this is the answer they want to take control of who to kill and when so far the royals object to them killing people they want

Meanwhile they can only harvest organs from criminals.

24 I'm we Ask what can be done then this is what can be done in my eyes it's time we turn the guns on the doctors they have crossed

ai e they are killing 6 months old babies just because they can they have become barbaric and worse when treatment has improved that makes us ask the real why this is the answer they have become traders of souls in Britain they harvest souls of the dead and use these to drive ever changing habits where real souls in acetate forms are given wriggling roerties to cause fabrication of flesh with severe results this has become the weapon for death how do we stop this we can simple ask acetate to eat away all this fibrosis acetate and chew the codes until they taste like bitter and ask to spit these up then job done

Now let's go back to be wearable book part we can see that the wearable books will make it hard for the people to imitate things but can make people act that way

Now if we Ask what can be done This is the answer we can always stop acetate development by a simple code like

acetate.destroy.develooment.start

But humans to live forever we need acetate in the correct format if we add too much then it become Aggressive if we add less then it becomes weak therefore what is the perfect amount needed for a human being is 789 which is also the frequency of God not sure if there is a coincidence or not if acetate is 789 then needed silkpasty is only 24 that means we live like God or its only I since I have God's image

To conclude we can see our Wearable Brain Books not just helping with learning but playing a major role in Medical Diagnosis as the Specialist this is something never possible without the discovery of Yahweh Anyone who said others is lying a perfect example is when the queen was tricked by Dr Alamos And the other silent Scottish killer doctor if someone else was listening meaning proof that they could go past everything to wearable books etc then they would have been stopped because our Wearable Brain Books link and synchronize and can be used to call for help.

Just think of the number 54 and see what happens

David Gomadza what do you want now

I am Queen Elizabeth and the Scottish are trying to kill me I am in Edinburgh they are using code 7958635210784 please find help forward message to the Prime Minister, M16 and the FBI all this to save taxpayers only. Am.

I not the one paying your salaries. After all Scottish must obey the British this is the state of things. Tell Me what can be done fast to stop these greedy Scottish. On behalf of Her Majest.

Communication Sign-out
Scottish fucks I send the army right now these swa…s must listen if I activate satellite I burn all in a flash don't they know [xrtuvwxyz - lockerbie bomber was Scottish. I covered that for them. A Scot assassinated a British Prime Minister?]
Background I just launched satellite and all the talk is to divert attention so that their brain can't ask the question whatdidhesay.start this is because brains will get an update using this question
Wearable Brain Books as Future tellers of the future
Just looking back on what we have covered already our prediction guided by our analysis has made us also Future Tellers or Sorcerers because we have predicted the future but our aim.is to save lives and change what is planned by others.

WEARABLE BRAIN BOOKS ARE THE FUTURE

THAT ARE READ DIRECTLY BY THE BRAIN AS OVERLAID ON THE
BRAIN OR EMBEDDED AND SAVED IN THE STERSTUVWXY WHERE BRAIN COMMANDS ARE USED TO UPLOAD, EMBED, READ, UNLOAD, SAVE AND REMOVE.

Our Invention New Brain Wearable Databases A New Way Of Reading Our Database Books.
Feel Our Books Through embedding and saving of nerve impulses and Action Potentials retrieving these and saving them in the auditory cortex and converting to correct form depending on whether a woman or a man.

FEEL OUR BOOKS TURN WORDS INTO FEELINGS

Nerve Impulses and Action Potentials.
Instead of reading using your eyes let your brain read of Database Books for you and turn words into feelings that is nerve impulses and Action Potentials through simple brain commands or actions.
You can simple tell your brain that you put the book [imaginary,] code xxxxx on your fingertips and you will flick it to wear it on your brain.
This means that training your brain to note actions like flicking fingers as wearing the book so that it can easily read it.

All our Databases are unique in that there is no one on earth that has written so many and so good above all no one on earth has ever used our Databases or any other the way we invented. All you need is a code we shall list in all our Databases
This code makes it easy for your brain to easily wear and read the Database
Above all you can simply embed all the information and convert it to Nerve Impulses and Action Potentials so that all you need is the right sense of humor to decode the information Let me take you through all you need to do
Above some don't even need a code but will simply with their hand pull the database from an imaginary location and fit it in your head
Now let's look how you can easily do this

1] say my brain is my reader

2] activate reading library

3] load Databases

4] search for David Gomadza

5] Thoughts To Word or Audio

6] Insert all Databases 1 to currently 44

7] Now Ask what if we could easily read all at once

8] say the end

Now what happens is a brief introduction but [might not be accurate do your own research on a topic because I write based on my belief about Yahweh God and my political orientation towards my own political party I founded; Tomorrow's World

Order www.twofuture.world

Now that is out of the way let's create codes for each Database in case you want to read just one book

Say open

Say close

Say open again

Say now close

These commands will help you maneuver easily

If we are to ask the brain a question it will be [how can you make reading a book fast and accurately] and this is the answer we get

Open a single Database at a time and write something on it first so that you can easily flip through the pages for example write

I want the best out of this Database

Now say

Save

Endorse Now

Space in

Start.End

Now Ask what can be improved

Your Database can be based on fiction as well not just facts some people don't want just the facts

Now say create a novels Database and add Evelina book series

These are the commands

Add Evelina book series by David Gomadza

Save

Endorse Now

Space In

Start.End [this is read as StartDotEnd]

Now Ask what is to be and what is the reply

Nothing is free one day I will put prices so be prepared to pay for the Databases up to £10 each or £2 for just reading it If you are happy say

OK

[From a certain date prices will go up after the free trial] Now that we have set up the Databases let's look at how we read these

Our brains are the most advanced systems on earth all you need is your brain and a code to read without using your eyes Now let's look in detail how this can be done Say to yourself loud I am the king. What happen?

I -The small right hand finger jerks am-The right hand thump jerks

The- Left thumb jersey

King - circle in the tongue

ALL OUR WEARABLE BRAIN BOOKS CODES

Now right down this code

82698

David Gomadza Databases [Thoughts To Word Or Audio]

Book 1 Code 76854

Book 2 code 789838

Book 3 code 7648381

Book 4 code 78984821

Book 5 code 867838692

Book 6 code 873898785

Book 7 code 889858321

Book 8 code 198385867

Book 9 code 38678982

Book 10 code 718598386

Book 11 code 71854321

Book 12 code 189867387

Book 13 code 7828519

Book 14 code 78389787

Book 15 code 28598678

Book 16 code 378928

Book 17 code 18487685

Book 18 code 12854367

Book 19 code 287641084

Book 20 code 38678185

Book 21 code 38788281

Book 22 code 285486718
Book 23 code7785987218
Book 24 code 7787613852
Book 25 code 187285876
Book 26 code 78218485
Book 27 code 3839785
Book 28 code 453848210
Book 29 code 287618410
Book 30 code 3878898274
Book 31 code 2811826789326
Book 32 code 85978284185
Book 33 code 86528118543202
Book 34 code 851918762850
Book 35 code 28788184828
Book 36 code 22185286110
Book 37 code 789767728418
Book 38 code 28778576385
Book 39 code 28678948358
Book 40 code 287289140
Book 41 code 28677898285
Book 42 code 19248517690
Book 43 code 772832198469
Book 44 code
Book 45 code 78986832154
Book 46 code 778598324180

HERE ARE THE BOOK TITLES

Book 1 Thoughts To Word or Audio
Book 2 Decoding the Brain Debunking the Misconceptions and Theories
Book 3 DATESTAMP:28 March 2022 Thoughts to Word or Audio. Volume III
Book 4 Genesis Brain Language Construction In Progress Book 5 Brain Code. The Benchmark of Decoding the Brain.
Book 6 How To Decode God, Creation, The Tree Of Life, Angels & Demons, The Devil, The Afterlife, The Underworld, The Brain, The Planets and The Universe.

Book 7 Brain Language Dictionary
Book 8 Encyclopedia of Decoding DNA sequence
Book 9 The Time Traveler. Back to the Assassination of Robert Kennedy
Book 10 Proof of Aliens on Mars. A Must Read If You Are Serious About Mars.
Book 11 How to make love to a woman
Book 12 As On Earth As In Heaven As It Is In Humans.
Book 13 Detailed Specification of the Decoding Device
Book 14 Detailed Specification Vol II
Book 15 The Electromagnetic Brain Waves Triangle
Book 16 Encyclopedia of Decoding the Brain 17 Decoding the Egyptian Pyramids
Book 18 Celebrities' Reset Switch. The 'Benjamin Button' Effect.
Book 19 Dictionary of The Codes Of Life
Book 20 Request For the Grant of a Patent
Book 21 A Brain Reader and A Brain Nerve Impulses
Book 22 Natural God Intelligence [NGI]. Brain-Peripherals-Databases-Interface [BPDI]
Book 23 Brain Action Potentials and their Corresponding Nerve Impulses
Book 24 Brain Codes. How The Brain Interprets The Universe In Numbers.
Book 25 Sabotage! By .trafficofficer. Tesla Car Accident on 27 February 2021.
Book 26 4 Brains Natural God Intelligence
Book 27 Genesis 2024 The Year of Increased Technological Advancement.
Book 28 Yahweh's Message
Book 29 Natural God Intelligence [NGI]. Brain-Peripherals-Databases-Interface [BPDI]
Book 30 Money for the Souls
Book 31 Brain Digital Decipher
Book 32 Brain Codes. How The Brain Interprets The Universe In Numbers.
Book 33 Body Codes. All and Everything in Numbers.
Book 34 Brain Power. How to Track and Kill your Enemies.
Book 35 Tomorrow's World Order Answering the critics

Book 36 Electromagnetic Waves Token
Book 37 Encyclopedia of Decoding Vision
Book 38 Ask 80 000 of Anything and The Laws of The Universe Will Give It to You. The Trick Behind All Cryptocurrency Heists.
Book 39 How To make Electrical Batteries That Lasts
Book 40 40 steps to make Any Woman have an Orgasm
Book 41 Encyclopedia of Decoding Vision. How the Brain Processes sight.
Books 42 Spicing, Arousing & Stimulating Things Up. 40 Steps to Make Any Woman Have an Orgasm.
Book 43 Encyclopedia of Decoding Speech. How the Brain Process Speech.
Book 44 Encyclopedia of Decoding Thinking. How the Brain thinks.
Book 45. Encyclopedia of Decoding Brain Senses. How the Brain Processes The Senses Of Touch, Sight, Hearing, Smell and Taste. Book 46 ALL HUMANS HAVE 4 BRAINS JUST AS GOD.
Now we can add Novels by me [David Gomadza]
Book 1 Evelina the Alpha code 8978685284
Book 2 Evelina the Omega code 77859838714
Book 3 Evelina God's Dilemma Solved code 78654329
Book 4 Evelina New World code 78654385
Now if we load all these this will complete the Database but there are some books by me [David Gomadza] which we can add also these are

1. Tomorrow's World Order code 7768528312
2. Tomorrow's World Order Dealing with the threats of invasion code 7819285765832
3. Evolution of Democracy 78983857159
4. The GreatShift 2023 code 78521908576
5. The Constitution. Tomorrow's World Order 7898385786790
6. Tomorrow's World Order Official Strategic Launch 7898385789240
7. All wars must end by June 2024 code 773876387498
8. Culling The sad reality of the IMF and World Bank loans as triggers of the law. code 9838578671564832
9. A perfect prediction Russia-Ukraine War Prediction code 7754879838572

10. An analysis of Evelina the novel series and the film scripts 1 code 7738598720285
11. Antitrust laws the case of Facebook v FTC code 779858764382
12. Russia and Ukraine's Peace Treaty code 77859823848
13. Mass Murder the West Behind the Pandemic and the Russia code 7798385789214
14. An order by the president of Tomorrow's World Order to send Peace keeping troop. ANSWERING 8776778921487

15.381 Days to Go. Russia-Ukraine War. code 99786431897210

16. Fortfied Defensive Training. Training to Build Massive Walls Around Vital Organs code 77983857218710
17. White paper Gtps.finance code 77285192876

18 Whitepaper Tomorrow's World Order code 9978483210687

19. New Single Reserve Global Currency code 789832185498
20. Direct Response to the Commission on Race and Ethnic Disparities Report. Code 789865418540
21. Irredeemable Annuities: The Slavery Abolishing Act Of 1833 code 778928385498267
22. The First Global President of the World's Russia-Ukraine Peace Plan. Code 6628591360828
23. COURT CASE DAVID GOMADZA/ TOMORROW'S WORLD ORDER V NHS, Great Britain. Code 77483899068523
24. CABAL SKRPT [1665-70s script] A Stories Prediction code 7789324892015
25. FREE JULIAN ASSANGE Escalate-to-De Escalate code 78983478237148
26. The Counter. As a Bargaining Tool. Code 778598324768510

Now if we are to load and unload a book these are the codes we need
Loading a book
Load Book code for example 786598321
Title How to Kill Your Enemies
Say
Load 786598321
[Loaded]
Then say open first page and read it
[chapter 1 and starts...]

To end reading
Say
End.start [means enddotstart]
Now add another
Say
Load new Book code 7768528312
Say
Open first page and read
To close
Say
Close
To end
Say
End.start [that is EnddotStart]
To unload
Say
Unload.
End.Start [Enddotstart]

There are some books that need to be converted to nerve impulses and Action Potentials so that you feel exactly what the book is talking about We have a good example;
40 Steps To Make Any Woman Have An Orgasm. Code 287289140
This is what you do to feel what the book is saying
Say
Load Book code 287289140
Embed in [sterstuvwxy] and unpack all nerve impulses and Action Potentials
[ready]
Now start the conversion where necessary to male from female
Now start
[5 minutes]
Message: Clitoris spark plugs not found
[Ignore and proceed without]
[Everything ready] OK
Start
[don't amplify anything]
[a lot of things missing like the create.hold.start and all the 21 squanks

if there a book with these codes?
Keep reading they are all in this book]
[You are right everything is here]

You must make sure that you are not near under 18s because they might feel what you feel Solution
Say create no under 18 of age triangle blockers and activate them code 98387648765823
Say Activate no under 18 code 98387648765823 and block every under 18 from reading this book or feeling it How to do it
[Add vicinity no under 18 only above 18 allowed] Activate code 98387648765823
Or create body electromagnetic waves emitter blocker that surrounds a person Say
Create a blocker of escaping electromagnetic waves from surrounding you
Code 7677893898432 for a man
Or 728923486790 for a woman
Now say
Activate 728924486890
[no one understands 18 will feel anything you are feeling]
How to read the book
Read.start
Read.page_.start eg read.page4.start
Now after to end
Say
End.start [that is enddotstart]
To undo embedding
Say
Undo the embedding of nerve impulses and Action Potentials This is the code
Undo.embednerveimpulses.actionpotentials.now.start
This will remove the embedded files
Now say Close
End.start
Sleep
But what if you don't want to remove the book and you want to keep it in your library then say,

Keep all files in the library
Keep.files.stersvwxy.start
Save
End.start
If you want to retrieve for example orgasm point only
Say
Retrieve climax feelings and save in the auditory cortex
Say
Retrieve.arousal.climax.save.auditorycortex.me
After a while say;
Activate.retrieved.files.convert.tonerveimpulse.start
End
Save
Start
Now
Ladies and gentlemen this is the future.
Feel a book as well. This is now possible

The End.

ABOUT DAVID GOMADZA

WWW.TWOFUTURE.WORLD

WHAT ARE WEARABLE BRAIN BOOKS?
Knowledge at the speed of thought
Choose a book. Get the corresponding code. Simply say, 'Upload & Read'. The Brain Converts Words into Nerve Impulses and Action Potentials So That You Feel The Books As Well.
PAPERBACK ISBN: 9798323522620

www.ingramcontent.com/pod-product-compliance
Lightning Source LLC
Chambersburg PA
CBHW051406250726
48656CB00006B/2296